Common to the Core
GUIDED JOURNAL FOR

ARTHIA NIXON

Common To The Core: Guided Journal For Teachers
Copyright © 2021 Arthia Nixon

Published by Royal Ambassador, LLC
Atlanta, Georgia

All rights reserved. No portion of this book may be reproduced in any form without permission from the publisher, except as permitted by U.S. copyright law.

Cover by Alejandra Stack & Canva

ISBN: 978-1-7349861-3-6

www.arthianixon.com

*This book is dedicated to every friend and relative of mine who has taught, especially those who continued to teach through COVID19. You are appreciated, you are loved, you are respected and you are honored.
Arkeria, Kieshla, Bernadette, Bodine, may your impact inspire.*

- Arthia Nixon

Dear Teacher,

You are where you thought you would be or are you? You came into this wanting to share your love of learning with the next generation of achievers and leaders. Now, you're in an environment you never anticipated you would be in.

Instead of simply worrying about disagreements in the classroom, you have to be on the lookout for signs of extreme bullying, fighting and potential shootings and more. Instead of pushing through the flu or a seasonal cold, you find yourself ensuring safety measures are being met as a global pandemic rages, hospitalizing some, killing others and shifting learning to trying to balance a virtually.

Some of your students will fail you, making you feel you have failed but everyday you continue, you are where you are meant to be.

Your primary duty is to teach students academic knowledge, but you are often the one who stands in as parents to them. You are the consistent example they see, the one they hope to earn praise from and often, your classroom may be the place of refuge they need.

You're also learning as you teach. What you do may seem only minimal for those who look on from the outside, but you should not let these views fret you. After all, you are the unsung advisor and contributor to the next generation.

It takes a lot for you to lower your pride and lengthen your patience for the sake of your pupils' betterment. It takes more to continue your education. It takes even more to sacrifice yourself, your free time and your family for the sake of your students.

Some of us substitute for a short time or teach on the short term. Some of us will never have what it takes to hang in for the long haul and so we tip our hats to you. Yet still, some of us are parents who teach and have to understand the fine balance between both in order to make a learner whole.

Teachers make a difference. You continue to do when others do not have the strength to go on. You continue to move forward and pull those behind you to keep up with you, while you also push those before you to continue to move further, and you hold those above you so that they would be stable at the level where they are. The world is grateful for how you teach your students. You are all the key to the future generation.

Reflections

WHAT WAS IT THAT MADE ME WANT TO BE A TEACHER?

WHICH TEACHER INSPIRED ME THE MOST AS A CHILD?

WHY DO I WANT TO CONTINUE TEACHING?

WHEN MY STUDENTS LEAVE MY CLASSROOM
I WANT THEM TO REMEMBER ME FOR:

Reflections

🍎 WHAT WAS IT THAT MADE ME WANT TO BE A TEACHER?

💡 WHICH TEACHER INSPIRED ME THE MOST AS A CHILD?

✏️ WHY DO I WANT TO CONTINUE TEACHING?

✈️ WHEN MY STUDENTS LEAVE MY CLASSROOM
I WANT THEM TO REMEMBER ME FOR:

Reflections

🍎 WHAT WAS IT THAT MADE ME WANT TO BE A TEACHER?

💡 WHICH TEACHER INSPIRED ME THE MOST AS A CHILD?

✏️ WHY DO I WANT TO CONTINUE TEACHING?

✈️ WHEN MY STUDENTS LEAVE MY CLASSROOM
I WANT THEM TO REMEMBER ME FOR:

> YOU CREATE THE CHANGE AND DIFFERENCE TO CREATE THE CHANGEMAKERS OF THE FUTURE WHO WILL MAKE THIS WORLD BETTER.

ARTHIA NIXON

Day #1

DATE:

I START EACH DAY WITH GRATITUDE

TODAY I AM GRATEFUL FOR ...

I KEEP MY FOCUS ON MY STUDENTS

MY GOAL FOR MY CLASS IS ...

FIVE THINGS I PLAN TO SHARE WITH MY STUDENTS TODAY

#1 ☐
#2 ☐
#3 ☐
#4 ☐
#5 ☐

SOMETHING MY STUDENT(S) DID TODAY I WANT TO REMEMBER

"

YOUR INFLUENCE DOES NOT STOP AFTER YOUR STUDENT GRADUATES, IT CONTINUES ON AND ON BEYOND THEIR GREATEST ACHIEVEMENTS.

"

ARTHIA NIXON

Day #2

DATE:

I START EACH DAY WITH GRATITUDE

TODAY I AM GRATEFUL FOR ...

I KEEP MY FOCUS ON MY STUDENTS

MY GOAL FOR MY CLASS IS ...

FIVE THINGS I PLAN TO SHARE WITH MY STUDENTS TODAY

#1 ☐
#2 ☐
#3 ☐
#4 ☐
#5 ☐

SOMETHING MY STUDENT(S) DID TODAY I WANT TO REMEMBER

"

FOR THE SCORES THAT WALK OUT
WITHOUT SAYING 'THANK YOU',
THERE WILL BE SOME WHO WILL TURN
BACK AND SHOW HOW MUCH THEY
APPRECIATE YOU.

"

ARTHIA NIXON

Day #3

DATE: _____

I START EACH DAY WITH GRATITUDE

TODAY I AM GRATEFUL FOR ...

_____

I KEEP MY FOCUS ON MY STUDENTS

MY GOAL FOR MY CLASS IS ...

_____
_____

FIVE THINGS I PLAN TO SHARE WITH MY STUDENTS TODAY

#1 _____ ☐
#2 _____ ☐
#3 _____ ☐
#4 _____ ☐
#5 _____ ☐

SOMETHING MY STUDENT(S) DID TODAY I WANT TO REMEMBER

_____
_____
_____
_____
_____

> SOME STUDENTS ARE HORRIBLE AND WILL MAKE YOU WANT TO QUIT. DO NOT FEEL GUILTY IF YOU DO. THAT MAY BE THE VERY THING THAT IS MEANT TO REDIRECT YOU TO WHERE YOU NEED TO BE.

ARTHIA NIXON

Day #4

DATE:

I START EACH DAY WITH GRATITUDE

TODAY I AM GRATEFUL FOR ...

I KEEP MY FOCUS ON MY STUDENTS

MY GOAL FOR MY CLASS IS ...

FIVE THINGS I PLAN TO SHARE WITH MY STUDENTS TODAY

#1 ☐
#2 ☐
#3 ☐
#4 ☐
#5 ☐

SOMETHING MY STUDENT(S) DID TODAY I WANT TO REMEMBER

> **IF YOU ARE GOING TO TEACH CHILDREN TO SPEAK UP FOR THEMSELVES, YOU WANT TO ENSURE YOU ARE PRACTICING THAT AS WELL.**

ARTHIA NIXON

Day #5

DATE:

I START EACH DAY WITH GRATITUDE

TODAY I AM GRATEFUL FOR ...

I KEEP MY FOCUS ON MY STUDENTS

MY GOAL FOR MY CLASS IS ...

FIVE THINGS I PLAN TO SHARE WITH MY STUDENTS TODAY

#1 ☐
#2 ☐
#3 ☐
#4 ☐
#5 ☐

SOMETHING MY STUDENT(S) DID TODAY I WANT TO REMEMBER

DO NOT CREATE A TOXIC ENVIRONMENT FOR YOUR COLLEAGUES. YOU NEED EACH OTHER TO COPE IN AND OUT OF THE CLASSROOM.

ARTHIA NIXON

DATE:

I START EACH DAY WITH GRATITUDE

TODAY I AM GRATEFUL FOR ...

I KEEP MY FOCUS ON MY STUDENTS

MY GOAL FOR MY CLASS IS ...

FIVE THINGS I PLAN TO SHARE WITH MY STUDENTS TODAY

#1 ☐
#2 ☐
#3 ☐
#4 ☐
#5 ☐

SOMETHING MY STUDENT(S) DID TODAY I WANT TO REMEMBER

"

IT DOESN'T END WHEN THE SCHOOL BELL RINGS. IT ENDS WHEN YOU NO LONGER HAVE THE ABILITY TO CONTINUE.

ARTHIA NIXON

Day #7

DATE:

I START EACH DAY WITH GRATITUDE

TODAY I AM GRATEFUL FOR ...

I KEEP MY FOCUS ON MY STUDENTS

MY GOAL FOR MY CLASS IS ...

FIVE THINGS I PLAN TO SHARE WITH MY STUDENTS TODAY

#1 ☐
#2 ☐
#3 ☐
#4 ☐
#5 ☐

SOMETHING MY STUDENT(S) DID TODAY I WANT TO REMEMBER

> **TODAY'S LESSONS SHAPE TOMORROW'S LEADERS**
>
> *ARTHIA NIXON*

Day #8

DATE:

I START EACH DAY WITH GRATITUDE

TODAY I AM GRATEFUL FOR ...

I KEEP MY FOCUS ON MY STUDENTS

MY GOAL FOR MY CLASS IS ...

FIVE THINGS I PLAN TO SHARE WITH MY STUDENTS TODAY

#1 ☐
#2 ☐
#3 ☐
#4 ☐
#5 ☐

SOMETHING MY STUDENT(S) DID TODAY I WANT TO REMEMBER

> **EVERYONE REMEMBERS THAT ONE TEACHER WHO MADE A DIFFERENCE IN THEIR LIFE AND WHO BELIEVED IN THEM. WHEN YOU WANT TO QUIT, REMEMBER, YOU ARE THE TEACHER SOMEONE WILL TALK ABOUT ONE DAY.**

ARTHIA NIXON

DATE:

I START EACH DAY WITH GRATITUDE

TODAY I AM GRATEFUL FOR ...

I KEEP MY FOCUS ON MY STUDENTS

MY GOAL FOR MY CLASS IS ...

FIVE THINGS I PLAN TO SHARE WITH MY STUDENTS TODAY

#1 ☐
#2 ☐
#3 ☐
#4 ☐
#5 ☐

SOMETHING MY STUDENT(S) DID TODAY I WANT TO REMEMBER

TODAY'S LESSONS SHAPE
TOMORROW'S LEADERS

ARTHIA NIXON

Day #10

DATE:

I START EACH DAY WITH GRATITUDE

TODAY I AM GRATEFUL FOR ...

I KEEP MY FOCUS ON MY STUDENTS

MY GOAL FOR MY CLASS IS ...

FIVE THINGS I PLAN TO SHARE WITH MY STUDENTS TODAY

#1 ☐
#2 ☐
#3 ☐
#4 ☐
#5 ☐

SOMETHING MY STUDENT(S) DID TODAY I WANT TO REMEMBER

> **YOUR ROAD AS A TEACHER MIGHT END WHEN YOU GET OLDER AND DIE, BUT YOUR INFLUENCE AS ONE WILL CONTINUE TO LIVE ON FOR ETERNITY.**

ARTHIA NIXON

Day #11

DATE:

| I START EACH DAY WITH GRATITUDE |

TODAY I AM GRATEFUL FOR ...

| I KEEP MY FOCUS ON MY STUDENTS |

MY GOAL FOR MY CLASS IS ...

| FIVE THINGS I PLAN TO SHARE WITH MY STUDENTS TODAY |

#1 ☐
#2 ☐
#3 ☐
#4 ☐
#5 ☐

| SOMETHING MY STUDENT(S) DID TODAY I WANT TO REMEMBER |

"

BEING A TEACHER IS MORE THAN GIVING A LESSON. IT IS BEING A PARENT, A MENTOR, A GUIDE AND MORE.

ARTHIA NIXON

Day #12

DATE:

I START EACH DAY WITH GRATITUDE

TODAY I AM GRATEFUL FOR ...

_____

I KEEP MY FOCUS ON MY STUDENTS

MY GOAL FOR MY CLASS IS ...

_____
_____

FIVE THINGS I PLAN TO SHARE WITH MY STUDENTS TODAY

#1 _____ ☐
#2 _____ ☐
#3 _____ ☐
#4 _____ ☐
#5 _____ ☐

SOMETHING MY STUDENT(S) DID TODAY I WANT TO REMEMBER

_____
_____
_____
_____

"

GETTING A STUDENT TO PASS THE CLASS IS NOT THE PRIMARY GOAL. THE GOAL IS TO CREATE A LIFELONG LEARNER.

ARTHIA NIXON

Day #13

DATE:

I START EACH DAY WITH GRATITUDE

TODAY I AM GRATEFUL FOR ...

I KEEP MY FOCUS ON MY STUDENTS

MY GOAL FOR MY CLASS IS ...

FIVE THINGS I PLAN TO SHARE WITH MY STUDENTS TODAY

#1 ☐
#2 ☐
#3 ☐
#4 ☐
#5 ☐

SOMETHING MY STUDENT(S) DID TODAY I WANT TO REMEMBER

"

EVERY CHILD LEARNS DIFFERENTLY. BE PATIENT. SOME MAY NOT HAVE THE BEST GRADES BUT THEY HAVE THE BEST HEARTS, BIGGEST TALENTS AND SKILLS BEYOND BELIEF. WE ARE ALL NEEDED TO COMPLETE THE PUZZLE.

"

ARTHIA NIXON

Day #14

DATE:

I START EACH DAY WITH GRATITUDE

TODAY I AM GRATEFUL FOR ...

I KEEP MY FOCUS ON MY STUDENTS

MY GOAL FOR MY CLASS IS ...

FIVE THINGS I PLAN TO SHARE WITH MY STUDENTS TODAY

#1 ☐
#2 ☐
#3 ☐
#4 ☐
#5 ☐

SOMETHING MY STUDENT(S) DID TODAY I WANT TO REMEMBER

> DO NOT BE THE TEACHER TO TELL A STUDENT TO QUIT ON SOMETHING THEY ARE PASSIONATE ABOUT. YOU MIGHT BE THE VERY ONE THEY NEED TO ENCOURAGE THEM TO PURSUE THAT PASSION IN ORDER FOR THEM TO FULFILL THEIR PURPOSE

ARTHIA NIXON

Day #15

DATE:

I START EACH DAY WITH GRATITUDE

TODAY I AM GRATEFUL FOR ...

I KEEP MY FOCUS ON MY STUDENTS

MY GOAL FOR MY CLASS IS ...

FIVE THINGS I PLAN TO SHARE WITH MY STUDENTS TODAY

#1 ☐
#2 ☐
#3 ☐
#4 ☐
#5 ☐

SOMETHING MY STUDENT(S) DID TODAY I WANT TO REMEMBER

"

JUST LIKE PARENTS, YOU SHAPE YOUR STUDENTS TO BECOME THE BEST THEY CAN BE BY BEING THE BEST THAT YOU ALREADY ARE.

ARTHIA NIXON

Day #16

DATE:

I START EACH DAY WITH GRATITUDE

TODAY I AM GRATEFUL FOR ...

I KEEP MY FOCUS ON MY STUDENTS

MY GOAL FOR MY CLASS IS ...

FIVE THINGS I PLAN TO SHARE WITH MY STUDENTS TODAY

#1 ☐
#2 ☐
#3 ☐
#4 ☐
#5 ☐

SOMETHING MY STUDENT(S) DID TODAY I WANT TO REMEMBER

"

YOU ARE UNDERPAID, OVERWORKED AND EXHAUSTED. DO NOT FEEL GUILTY FOR PRACTICING YOUR SELF-CARE IN ORDER TO BETTER SERVE YOURSEL AND YOUR STUDENTS.

"

ARTHIA NIXON

Day #17

DATE:

I START EACH DAY WITH GRATITUDE

TODAY I AM GRATEFUL FOR ...

I KEEP MY FOCUS ON MY STUDENTS

MY GOAL FOR MY CLASS IS ...

FIVE THINGS I PLAN TO SHARE WITH MY STUDENTS TODAY

#1 ☐
#2 ☐
#3 ☐
#4 ☐
#5 ☐

SOMETHING MY STUDENT(S) DID TODAY I WANT TO REMEMBER

> YOU DO NOT GIVE YOUR STUDENTS ANSWERS. YOU TEACH THEM TO LEARN HOW TO THINK FOR THEMSELVES.

— ARTHIA NIXON

Day #18

DATE:

I START EACH DAY WITH GRATITUDE

TODAY I AM GRATEFUL FOR ...

I KEEP MY FOCUS ON MY STUDENTS

MY GOAL FOR MY CLASS IS ...

FIVE THINGS I PLAN TO SHARE WITH MY STUDENTS TODAY

#1 ☐
#2 ☐
#3 ☐
#4 ☐
#5 ☐

SOMETHING MY STUDENT(S) DID TODAY I WANT TO REMEMBER

"

TEACHERS NOT ONLY LOVE TO TEACH AND LEARN, THEY ALSO LOVE THE TEACHERS AND LEARNERS.

ARTHIA NIXON

Day #19

DATE:

I START EACH DAY WITH GRATITUDE

TODAY I AM GRATEFUL FOR ...

I KEEP MY FOCUS ON MY STUDENTS

MY GOAL FOR MY CLASS IS ...

FIVE THINGS I PLAN TO SHARE WITH MY STUDENTS TODAY

#1 ☐
#2 ☐
#3 ☐
#4 ☐
#5 ☐

SOMETHING MY STUDENT(S) DID TODAY I WANT TO REMEMBER

"

TEACHING MAY BE CONSIDERED ONE SINGLE PROFESSION, BUT OVERALL, TEACHING SERVES AS THE FERTILE GROUND TO CULTIVATE COUNTLESS VOCATIONS.

ARTHIA NIXON

Day #20

DATE:

I START EACH DAY WITH GRATITUDE

TODAY I AM GRATEFUL FOR ...

I KEEP MY FOCUS ON MY STUDENTS

MY GOAL FOR MY CLASS IS ...

FIVE THINGS I PLAN TO SHARE WITH MY STUDENTS TODAY

#1 ☐
#2 ☐
#3 ☐
#4 ☐
#5 ☐

SOMETHING MY STUDENT(S) DID TODAY I WANT TO REMEMBER

"

YOU MAY BE BURNING OUT, BUT LIKE A CANDLE, YOU ARE THE BEACON YOUR STUDENTS NEED TO BE GUIDED ON THEIR WAY.

ARTHIA NIXON

Day #21

DATE:

I START EACH DAY WITH GRATITUDE

TODAY I AM GRATEFUL FOR ...

I KEEP MY FOCUS ON MY STUDENTS

MY GOAL FOR MY CLASS IS ...

FIVE THINGS I PLAN TO SHARE WITH MY STUDENTS TODAY

#1 ☐
#2 ☐
#3 ☐
#4 ☐
#5 ☐

SOMETHING MY STUDENT(S) DID TODAY I WANT TO REMEMBER

"

YOU ARE NOT MERELY TEACHING,
YOU ARE INFLUENCING AND
INSTILLING.

"

ARTHIA NIXON

Day #22

DATE:

I START EACH DAY WITH GRATITUDE

TODAY I AM GRATEFUL FOR ...

I KEEP MY FOCUS ON MY STUDENTS

MY GOAL FOR MY CLASS IS ...

FIVE THINGS I PLAN TO SHARE WITH MY STUDENTS TODAY

#1 ☐
#2 ☐
#3 ☐
#4 ☐
#5 ☐

SOMETHING MY STUDENT(S) DID TODAY I WANT TO REMEMBER

"

BECAUSE OF YOU, MANY ARE THE
SUCCESSFUL PERSONS THAT
CONTINUOUSLY BRING CHANGE TO
THE WORLD.

ARTHIA NIXON

Day #23

DATE:

I START EACH DAY WITH GRATITUDE

TODAY I AM GRATEFUL FOR ...

I KEEP MY FOCUS ON MY STUDENTS

MY GOAL FOR MY CLASS IS ...

FIVE THINGS I PLAN TO SHARE WITH MY STUDENTS TODAY

#1
#2
#3
#4
#5

SOMETHING MY STUDENT(S) DID TODAY I WANT TO REMEMBER

"

NO PRESSURE, BUT YOU ARE NOT JUST TEACHING A CHILD. YOU ARE THE FIRST ADVISOR TO TOMORROW'S NEXT PRESIDENT, PRIME MINISTER, POPE, CEO AND LEADER.

ARTHIA NIXON

Day #24

DATE:

I START EACH DAY WITH GRATITUDE

TODAY I AM GRATEFUL FOR ...

I KEEP MY FOCUS ON MY STUDENTS

MY GOAL FOR MY CLASS IS ...

FIVE THINGS I PLAN TO SHARE WITH MY STUDENTS TODAY

#1 ☐
#2 ☐
#3 ☐
#4 ☐
#5 ☐

SOMETHING MY STUDENT(S) DID TODAY I WANT TO REMEMBER

> **EDUCATING SOMEONE IS NOT TO MAKE THEIR LIVES BETTER, BUT EDUCATION, ITSELF, IS CREATING A BETTER LIFE.**

ARTHIA NIXON

Day #25

DATE:

I START EACH DAY WITH GRATITUDE

TODAY I AM GRATEFUL FOR ...

I KEEP MY FOCUS ON MY STUDENTS

MY GOAL FOR MY CLASS IS ...

FIVE THINGS I PLAN TO SHARE WITH MY STUDENTS TODAY

#1 ☐
#2 ☐
#3 ☐
#4 ☐
#5 ☐

SOMETHING MY STUDENT(S) DID TODAY I WANT TO REMEMBER

"
YOU DON'T JUST SHAPE A CHILD, YOU ALSO ARE A PART OF SHAPING THAT CHILD'S FUTURE AND THE FUTURE AS A WHOLE.
"

ARTHIA NIXON

Day #26

DATE:

I START EACH DAY WITH GRATITUDE

TODAY I AM GRATEFUL FOR ...

I KEEP MY FOCUS ON MY STUDENTS

MY GOAL FOR MY CLASS IS ...

FIVE THINGS I PLAN TO SHARE WITH MY STUDENTS TODAY

#1 ☐
#2 ☐
#3 ☐
#4 ☐
#5 ☐

SOMETHING MY STUDENT(S) DID TODAY I WANT TO REMEMBER

> **LEARNING IS BOTH TEACHING AND APPLYING. IF YOUR STUDENTS ARE LEARNING, THEY ARE REMEMBERING AND ARE INFLUENCED BY WHAT YOU TEACH THEM.**

ARTHIA NIXON

Day #27

DATE:

I START EACH DAY WITH GRATITUDE

TODAY I AM GRATEFUL FOR ...

I KEEP MY FOCUS ON MY STUDENTS

MY GOAL FOR MY CLASS IS ...

FIVE THINGS I PLAN TO SHARE WITH MY STUDENTS TODAY

#1
#2
#3
#4
#5

SOMETHING MY STUDENT(S) DID TODAY I WANT TO REMEMBER

> "SCHOOL CAN SOMETIMES BE THE REFUGE CHILDREN NEED TO GET AWAY FROM THE WAR AT HOME. A TEACHER MIGHT BE THE SAVIOR THEY NEED TO SPEAK UP ON THEIR BEHALF."

— ARTHIA NIXON

Day #28

DATE:

I START EACH DAY WITH GRATITUDE

TODAY I AM GRATEFUL FOR ...

I KEEP MY FOCUS ON MY STUDENTS

MY GOAL FOR MY CLASS IS ...

FIVE THINGS I PLAN TO SHARE WITH MY STUDENTS TODAY

#1 ☐
#2 ☐
#3 ☐
#4 ☐
#5 ☐

SOMETHING MY STUDENT(S) DID TODAY I WANT TO REMEMBER

"

DO NOT BE THE TEACHER TO TELL A STUDENT TO QUIT ON SOMETHING THEY ARE PASSIONATE ABOUT. YOU MIGHT BE THE VERY ONE THEY NEED TO ENCOURAGE THEM TO PURSUE THAT PASSION IN ORDER FOR THEM TO FULFILL THEIR PURPOSE

ARTHIA NIXON

Day #29

DATE:

I START EACH DAY WITH GRATITUDE

TODAY I AM GRATEFUL FOR ...

I KEEP MY FOCUS ON MY STUDENTS

MY GOAL FOR MY CLASS IS ...

FIVE THINGS I PLAN TO SHARE WITH MY STUDENTS TODAY

#1 ☐
#2 ☐
#3 ☐
#4 ☐
#5 ☐

SOMETHING MY STUDENT(S) DID TODAY I WANT TO REMEMBER

> **BEING AN EFFECTIVE TEACHER IS NOT JUST SEEING YOUR STUDENTS' CORRECT ANSWERS, BUT IT IS SEEING AND LISTENING WHEN YOUR STUDENTS HAVE QUESTIONS.**

ARTHIA NIXON

Day #30

DATE:

I START EACH DAY WITH GRATITUDE

TODAY I AM GRATEFUL FOR …

I KEEP MY FOCUS ON MY STUDENTS

MY GOAL FOR MY CLASS IS …

FIVE THINGS I PLAN TO SHARE WITH MY STUDENTS TODAY

- #1 ☐
- #2 ☐
- #3 ☐
- #4 ☐
- #5 ☐

SOMETHING MY STUDENT(S) DID TODAY I WANT TO REMEMBER

"

YOU DON'T REALIZE THE IMPACT YOU ARE MAKING WHILE YOU ARE MAKING THE IMPACT. YOU WILL SEE THE IMPACT WHEN IT IS REVEALED IN THE FUTURE ADULTS WHO CREDIT YOU FOR IMPACTING THEM.

ARTHIA NIXON

Day #31

DATE:

I START EACH DAY WITH GRATITUDE

TODAY I AM GRATEFUL FOR ...

I KEEP MY FOCUS ON MY STUDENTS

MY GOAL FOR MY CLASS IS ...

FIVE THINGS I PLAN TO SHARE WITH MY STUDENTS TODAY

#1 ☐
#2 ☐
#3 ☐
#4 ☐
#5 ☐

SOMETHING MY STUDENT(S) DID TODAY I WANT TO REMEMBER

> **THE LESSONS YOU CREATE DO NOT LAST FOR A PERIOD. THEY LAST A LIFETIME.**

ARTHIA NIXON

Day #32

DATE:

I START EACH DAY WITH GRATITUDE

TODAY I AM GRATEFUL FOR ...

I KEEP MY FOCUS ON MY STUDENTS

MY GOAL FOR MY CLASS IS ...

FIVE THINGS I PLAN TO SHARE WITH MY STUDENTS TODAY

#1 ☐
#2 ☐
#3 ☐
#4 ☐
#5 ☐

SOMETHING MY STUDENT(S) DID TODAY I WANT TO REMEMBER

 DATE:

I START EACH DAY WITH GRATITUDE

TODAY I AM GRATEFUL FOR ...

I KEEP MY FOCUS ON MY STUDENTS

MY GOAL FOR MY CLASS IS ...

FIVE THINGS I PLAN TO SHARE WITH MY STUDENTS TODAY

#1 ☐
#2 ☐
#3 ☐
#4 ☐
#5 ☐

SOMETHING MY STUDENT(S) DID TODAY I WANT TO REMEMBER

Day #34

DATE:

I START EACH DAY WITH GRATITUDE

TODAY I AM GRATEFUL FOR ...

I KEEP MY FOCUS ON MY STUDENTS

MY GOAL FOR MY CLASS IS ...

FIVE THINGS I PLAN TO SHARE WITH MY STUDENTS TODAY

#1 ☐
#2 ☐
#3 ☐
#4 ☐
#5 ☐

SOMETHING MY STUDENT(S) DID TODAY I WANT TO REMEMBER

Day #35

DATE:

I START EACH DAY WITH GRATITUDE

TODAY I AM GRATEFUL FOR ...

I KEEP MY FOCUS ON MY STUDENTS

MY GOAL FOR MY CLASS IS ...

FIVE THINGS I PLAN TO SHARE WITH MY STUDENTS TODAY

#1 ☐
#2 ☐
#3 ☐
#4 ☐
#5 ☐

SOMETHING MY STUDENT(S) DID TODAY I WANT TO REMEMBER

Day #36

DATE:

I START EACH DAY WITH GRATITUDE

TODAY I AM GRATEFUL FOR ...

I KEEP MY FOCUS ON MY STUDENTS

MY GOAL FOR MY CLASS IS ...

FIVE THINGS I PLAN TO SHARE WITH MY STUDENTS TODAY

#1 ☐
#2 ☐
#3 ☐
#4 ☐
#5 ☐

SOMETHING MY STUDENT(S) DID TODAY I WANT TO REMEMBER

Day #37

DATE:

I START EACH DAY WITH GRATITUDE

TODAY I AM GRATEFUL FOR ...

I KEEP MY FOCUS ON MY STUDENTS

MY GOAL FOR MY CLASS IS ...

FIVE THINGS I PLAN TO SHARE WITH MY STUDENTS TODAY

#1
#2
#3
#4
#5

 SOMETHING MY STUDENT(S) DID TODAY I WANT TO REMEMBER

Day #38

DATE: _____

I START EACH DAY WITH GRATITUDE

TODAY I AM GRATEFUL FOR ...

_____

I KEEP MY FOCUS ON MY STUDENTS

MY GOAL FOR MY CLASS IS ...

_____
_____

FIVE THINGS I PLAN TO SHARE WITH MY STUDENTS TODAY

#1 _____ ☐
#2 _____ ☐
#3 _____ ☐
#4 _____ ☐
#5 _____ ☐

SOMETHING MY STUDENT(S) DID TODAY I WANT TO REMEMBER

_____
_____
_____
_____
_____

Day #39

DATE:

I START EACH DAY WITH GRATITUDE

TODAY I AM GRATEFUL FOR ...

I KEEP MY FOCUS ON MY STUDENTS

MY GOAL FOR MY CLASS IS ...

FIVE THINGS I PLAN TO SHARE WITH MY STUDENTS TODAY

#1
#2
#3
#4
#5

SOMETHING MY STUDENT(S) DID TODAY I WANT TO REMEMBER

Day #40

DATE:

I START EACH DAY WITH GRATITUDE

TODAY I AM GRATEFUL FOR ...

I KEEP MY FOCUS ON MY STUDENTS

MY GOAL FOR MY CLASS IS ...

FIVE THINGS I PLAN TO SHARE WITH MY STUDENTS TODAY

#1 ☐
#2 ☐
#3 ☐
#4 ☐
#5 ☐

SOMETHING MY STUDENT(S) DID TODAY I WANT TO REMEMBER

Day #41

DATE:

I START EACH DAY WITH GRATITUDE

TODAY I AM GRATEFUL FOR ...

I KEEP MY FOCUS ON MY STUDENTS

MY GOAL FOR MY CLASS IS ...

FIVE THINGS I PLAN TO SHARE WITH MY STUDENTS TODAY

#1 ☐
#2 ☐
#3 ☐
#4 ☐
#5 ☐

SOMETHING MY STUDENT(S) DID TODAY I WANT TO REMEMBER

Day #42

DATE:

I START EACH DAY WITH GRATITUDE

TODAY I AM GRATEFUL FOR ...

I KEEP MY FOCUS ON MY STUDENTS

MY GOAL FOR MY CLASS IS ...

FIVE THINGS I PLAN TO SHARE WITH MY STUDENTS TODAY

#1 ☐
#2 ☐
#3 ☐
#4 ☐
#5 ☐

SOMETHING MY STUDENT(S) DID TODAY I WANT TO REMEMBER

Day #43

DATE:

I START EACH DAY WITH GRATITUDE

TODAY I AM GRATEFUL FOR ...

I KEEP MY FOCUS ON MY STUDENTS

MY GOAL FOR MY CLASS IS ...

FIVE THINGS I PLAN TO SHARE WITH MY STUDENTS TODAY

#1 ☐
#2 ☐
#3 ☐
#4 ☐
#5 ☐

SOMETHING MY STUDENT(S) DID TODAY I WANT TO REMEMBER

Day #44

DATE:

I START EACH DAY WITH GRATITUDE

TODAY I AM GRATEFUL FOR ...

I KEEP MY FOCUS ON MY STUDENTS

MY GOAL FOR MY CLASS IS ...

FIVE THINGS I PLAN TO SHARE WITH MY STUDENTS TODAY

#1 ☐
#2 ☐
#3 ☐
#4 ☐
#5 ☐

SOMETHING MY STUDENT(S) DID TODAY I WANT TO REMEMBER

Day #45

DATE:

I START EACH DAY WITH GRATITUDE

TODAY I AM GRATEFUL FOR …

I KEEP MY FOCUS ON MY STUDENTS

MY GOAL FOR MY CLASS IS …

FIVE THINGS I PLAN TO SHARE WITH MY STUDENTS TODAY

- #1 ☐
- #2 ☐
- #3 ☐
- #4 ☐
- #5 ☐

SOMETHING MY STUDENT(S) DID TODAY I WANT TO REMEMBER

Day #46

DATE:

I START EACH DAY WITH GRATITUDE

TODAY I AM GRATEFUL FOR ...

I KEEP MY FOCUS ON MY STUDENTS

MY GOAL FOR MY CLASS IS ...

FIVE THINGS I PLAN TO SHARE WITH MY STUDENTS TODAY

#1 ☐
#2 ☐
#3 ☐
#4 ☐
#5 ☐

SOMETHING MY STUDENT(S) DID TODAY I WANT TO REMEMBER

Day #47

DATE:

I START EACH DAY WITH GRATITUDE

TODAY I AM GRATEFUL FOR ...

I KEEP MY FOCUS ON MY STUDENTS

MY GOAL FOR MY CLASS IS ...

FIVE THINGS I PLAN TO SHARE WITH MY STUDENTS TODAY

#1 ☐
#2 ☐
#3 ☐
#4 ☐
#5 ☐

SOMETHING MY STUDENT(S) DID TODAY I WANT TO REMEMBER

Day #48

DATE:

I START EACH DAY WITH GRATITUDE

TODAY I AM GRATEFUL FOR ...

I KEEP MY FOCUS ON MY STUDENTS

MY GOAL FOR MY CLASS IS ...

FIVE THINGS I PLAN TO SHARE WITH MY STUDENTS TODAY

#1 ☐
#2 ☐
#3 ☐
#4 ☐
#5 ☐

SOMETHING MY STUDENT(S) DID TODAY I WANT TO REMEMBER

Day #49

DATE:

I START EACH DAY WITH GRATITUDE

TODAY I AM GRATEFUL FOR ...

I KEEP MY FOCUS ON MY STUDENTS

MY GOAL FOR MY CLASS IS ...

FIVE THINGS I PLAN TO SHARE WITH MY STUDENTS TODAY

#1 ☐
#2 ☐
#3 ☐
#4 ☐
#5 ☐

SOMETHING MY STUDENT(S) DID TODAY I WANT TO REMEMBER

# Day #50

DATE:

I START EACH DAY WITH GRATITUDE

TODAY I AM GRATEFUL FOR …

I KEEP MY FOCUS ON MY STUDENTS

MY GOAL FOR MY CLASS IS …

FIVE THINGS I PLAN TO SHARE WITH MY STUDENTS TODAY

#1 ☐
#2 ☐
#3 ☐
#4 ☐
#5 ☐

SOMETHING MY STUDENT(S) DID TODAY I WANT TO REMEMBER

My Thoughts

My Thoughts

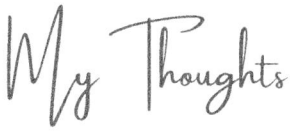

My Thoughts

www.ingramcontent.com/pod-product-compliance
Lightning Source LLC
Chambersburg PA
CBHW060206050426
42446CB00013B/3004